TRADI PARAGUAYAN COOKBOOK

AVA BAKER

CONTENTS

SNACKS 60

DESSERTS 79

APPETIZERS

Chipa (Cheese and Cornmeal Bread)

Servings: 12-15

Time: 45 minutes

Ingredients:

- 3 cups cornmeal
- 2 cups tapioca starch
- 1 cup butter, melted
- 1 cup milk
- 3 eggs
- 2 cups grated Paraguayan cheese (Queso Paraguay)
- 1 tablespoon anise seeds
- 1 teaspoon salt

Directions:

1. Preheat the oven to 350°F (180°C). Grease a baking sheet.

2. In a large bowl, mix cornmeal, tapioca starch, and salt.

3. In a saucepan, heat milk and butter until melted. Add to the dry ingredients and mix well.

4. Add eggs one at a time, stirring after each addition.

5. Fold in the grated cheese and anise seeds until the dough is well combined.

6. With moistened hands, shape the dough into small rounds or traditional crescent shapes.

7. Place on the greased baking sheet and bake for 25-30 minutes or until golden brown.

8. Allow Chipa to cool slightly before serving.

Sopa Paraguaya (Paraguayan Cornbread Soup)

Servings: 6-8

Time: 1 hour

Ingredients:

- 2 cups cornmeal
- 2 cups whole milk
- 4 cups chicken or vegetable broth
- 1 cup grated Paraguayan cheese (Queso Paraguay)
- 1 cup onions, finely chopped
- 1 cup bell peppers, finely chopped
- 1/2 cup butter, melted
- 4 eggs
- Salt and pepper to taste

Directions:

1. Preheat the oven to 375°F (190°C). Grease a baking dish.
2. In a large mixing bowl, combine cornmeal, milk, and melted butter. Mix until well combined.
3. In a separate pan, sauté onions and bell peppers until tender. Add them to the cornmeal mixture.
4. Beat the eggs and add them to the mixture, stirring well.

5. Gradually add the chicken or vegetable broth, stirring continuously to avoid lumps.

6. Fold in the grated cheese and season with salt and pepper.

7. Pour the mixture into the greased baking dish and bake for 30-40 minutes or until golden brown and set.

8. Allow Sopa Paraguaya to cool slightly before serving.

Mandioca Frita (Fried Cassava)

Servings: 4-6

Time: 30 minutes

Ingredients:

- 2 pounds cassava (mandioca), peeled and cut into sticks
- Vegetable oil for frying
- Salt to taste

Directions:

1. Rinse the cassava sticks under cold water to remove excess starch.
2. In a large pot, bring water to a boil and add cassava sticks. Cook for about 10-15 minutes or until they are just fork-tender.
3. Remove cassava from the pot and let them cool slightly.
4. Heat vegetable oil in a deep fryer or large skillet to 350°F (175°C).
5. Carefully place the cassava sticks into the hot oil, frying in batches until golden brown and crispy.
6. Using a slotted spoon, transfer the fried cassava to a paper towel-lined plate to drain excess oil.
7. Sprinkle with salt while still hot and toss to coat evenly.

Empanadas Paraguayas (Paraguayan Empanadas)

Servings: 10

Time: 1 hour

Ingredients:

- 2 cups all-purpose flour
- 1 cup warm water
- 1/4 cup lard or vegetable shortening
- 1 teaspoon salt
- 1 pound ground beef
- 1 onion, finely chopped
- 1 bell pepper, finely chopped
- 2 hard-boiled eggs, chopped
- 1/2 cup green olives, pitted and sliced
- 1 teaspoon cumin
- Salt and pepper to taste
- Vegetable oil for frying

Directions:

1. In a large bowl, mix flour, warm water, lard (or vegetable shortening), and salt to form a smooth dough. Let it rest for 30 minutes.

2. In a skillet, cook ground beef over medium heat until browned. Add onions and bell peppers, cooking until vegetables are tender.

3. Stir in cumin, salt, and pepper. Remove from heat and let it cool.

4. Preheat vegetable oil in a deep fryer or large skillet to 350°F (175°C).

5. Roll out the dough on a floured surface and cut circles (about 6 inches in diameter).

6. Spoon a portion of the meat mixture onto each dough circle. Add chopped hard-boiled eggs and sliced olives.

7. Fold the dough over the filling, forming a half-moon shape, and seal the edges by pressing with a fork.

8. Fry the empanadas in batches until golden brown on both sides.

9. Drain on a paper towel-lined plate and serve hot.

Pastel Mandi'o (Cassava Dumplings)

Servings: 6-8

Time: 45 minutes

Ingredients:

- 2 cups cassava (mandioca), grated
- 1 cup cornstarch
- 1 egg
- 1/2 cup grated Paraguayan cheese (Queso Paraguay)
- 1/4 cup green onions, finely chopped
- Salt to taste
- Vegetable oil for frying

Directions:

1. In a large bowl, combine grated cassava, cornstarch, and salt.
2. Add the egg, grated cheese, and chopped green onions to the cassava mixture. Mix until well combined.
3. Take a portion of the mixture and shape it into a small, flat dumpling.
4. Heat vegetable oil in a deep fryer or large skillet to 350°F (175°C).
5. Carefully place the cassava dumplings into the hot oil, frying until they turn golden brown and crispy.

6. Use a slotted spoon to remove the dumplings from the oil and place them on a paper towel-lined plate to drain excess oil.

Albóndigas a la Paraguaya (Paraguayan Meatballs)

Servings: 4-6

Time: 1 hour

Ingredients:

- 1 pound ground beef
- 1/2 cup cooked rice
- 1/4 cup cornmeal
- 1 onion, finely chopped
- 2 cloves garlic, minced
- 1/4 cup fresh parsley, chopped
- 1 teaspoon ground cumin
- 1 teaspoon paprika
- Salt and pepper to taste
- 1 egg
- Vegetable oil for frying

Directions:

1. In a large mixing bowl, combine ground beef, cooked rice, cornmeal, chopped onion, minced garlic, parsley, cumin, paprika, salt, and pepper.

2. Beat the egg and add it to the mixture. Mix until well combined.

3. Shape the mixture into golf ball-sized meatballs.

4. Heat vegetable oil in a large skillet over medium heat.

5. Fry the meatballs until golden brown on all sides, ensuring they are cooked through.

6. Remove the meatballs from the skillet and place them on a paper towel-lined plate to absorb excess oil.

Mbejú (Cheese and Cassava Pancake)

Servings: 4-6

Time: 45 minutes

Ingredients:

- 2 cups cassava flour
- 1 cup whole milk
- 1 cup grated Paraguayan cheese (Queso Paraguay)
- 1/2 cup butter, melted
- 2 eggs
- Salt to taste

Directions:

1. In a mixing bowl, combine cassava flour, grated cheese, and a pinch of salt.
2. In a saucepan, heat the milk and butter until the butter is melted. Add this mixture to the dry ingredients and mix well.
3. Beat the eggs and add them to the batter, stirring until smooth.
4. Heat a non-stick skillet or griddle over medium heat.
5. Pour a ladleful of batter onto the skillet, spreading it thinly to form a pancake.

6. Cook until the edges are golden brown, then flip and cook the other side until done.

7. Repeat the process with the remaining batter.

Puchero Paraguayo (Paraguayan Stew)

Servings: 6-8

Time: 2 hours

Ingredients:

- 1 pound beef stew meat, cubed
- 1 cup smoked sausage, sliced
- 1 cup pork ribs
- 1 cup butternut squash, peeled and diced
- 1 cup sweet potatoes, peeled and diced
- 1 cup corn on the cob, cut into thirds
- 1 cup green beans, trimmed
- 1 onion, chopped
- 2 cloves garlic, minced
- 2 tomatoes, diced
- 1 bell pepper, diced
- 1 teaspoon dried oregano
- Salt and pepper to taste
- 8 cups water or beef broth

Directions:

1. In a large pot, combine beef stew meat, smoked sausage, and pork ribs. Cover with water or beef broth and bring to a boil.

2. Skim off any foam that rises to the surface, then reduce heat to simmer.

3. Add butternut squash, sweet potatoes, corn on the cob, and green beans to the pot.

4. In a separate pan, sauté onions, garlic, tomatoes, and bell peppers until softened. Add this mixture to the pot.

5. Season with dried oregano, salt, and pepper. Stir well.

6. Simmer the stew for 1.5 to 2 hours or until the meat is tender and the vegetables are cooked.

Torta de So'o (Paraguayan Beef Pie)

Servings: 8-10

Time: 1.5 hours

Ingredients:

- 1 pound ground beef
- 1 onion, finely chopped
- 2 bell peppers, diced
- 2 tomatoes, diced
- 1/2 cup green olives, pitted and sliced
- 1 hard-boiled egg, chopped
- 1 cup corn kernels (fresh or frozen)
- 2 tablespoons vegetable oil
- Salt and pepper to taste
- 2 cups all-purpose flour
- 1 cup butter, cold and cubed
- 1/4 cup ice-cold water

Directions:

1. In a skillet, heat vegetable oil over medium heat. Add ground beef and cook until browned.
2. Add chopped onions and bell peppers, sautéing until vegetables are tender.

3. Stir in diced tomatoes, green olives, chopped hard-boiled egg, and corn kernels. Season with salt and pepper. Set aside.

4. In a large mixing bowl, combine all-purpose flour and cubed butter. Use your fingers or a pastry cutter to incorporate the butter until the mixture resembles coarse crumbs.

5. Gradually add ice-cold water, mixing until the dough comes together.

6. Divide the dough into two portions: one for the base and one for the top crust.

7. Roll out the larger portion and line a pie dish with the dough.

8. Spoon the beef filling onto the crust and spread evenly.

9. Roll out the remaining dough to create the top crust. Place it over the filling and seal the edges.

10. Cut a few slits in the top crust to allow steam to escape.

11. Bake the Torta de So'o in a preheated oven at 375°F (190°C) for 30-40 minutes or until the crust is golden brown.

12. Allow it to cool slightly before slicing.

Sopa de Maní (Peanut Soup)

Servings: 4-6

Time: 1 hour

Ingredients:

- 1 cup roasted peanuts, unsalted
- 1 onion, finely chopped
- 2 cloves garlic, minced
- 2 tablespoons vegetable oil
- 1 cup tomatoes, diced
- 1 bell pepper, diced
- 1 carrot, peeled and sliced
- 1 sweet potato, peeled and diced
- 1 cup pumpkin, peeled and diced
- 6 cups vegetable or chicken broth
- 1 teaspoon ground cumin
- Salt and pepper to taste
- Fresh cilantro, chopped (for garnish)

Directions:

1. In a blender, pulse the roasted peanuts until finely ground. Set aside.

2. In a large pot, heat vegetable oil over medium heat. Add chopped onions and minced garlic, sautéing until fragrant.

3. Add diced tomatoes, bell peppers, sliced carrots, sweet potatoes, and pumpkin to the pot. Cook for 5-7 minutes until vegetables begin to soften.

4. Pour in the vegetable or chicken broth and bring the mixture to a boil.

5. Stir in the ground peanuts and reduce heat to simmer. Cook for an additional 30-40 minutes or until the vegetables are tender.

6. Season with ground cumin, salt, and pepper to taste. Adjust seasoning as needed.

7. Allow the soup to cool slightly before serving.

8. Garnish with chopped fresh cilantro and serve Sopa de Maní hot.

MAIN COURSES

Asado Paraguayo (Paraguayan Barbecue)

Servings: 4-6

Time: 2-3 hours (including marination)

Ingredients:

- 2 pounds beef short ribs
- 1 cup chimichurri sauce (see recipe below)
- Salt and pepper to taste

Chimichurri Sauce:

- 1 cup fresh parsley, finely chopped
- 1/2 cup fresh oregano leaves, finely chopped
- 4 cloves garlic, minced
- 1 teaspoon red pepper flakes

- 1/2 cup red wine vinegar
- 1 cup extra-virgin olive oil
- Salt and pepper to taste

Directions:

1. Season the beef short ribs with salt and pepper, ensuring an even coating.
2. In a bowl, mix together the ingredients for the chimichurri sauce: parsley, oregano, garlic, red pepper flakes, red wine vinegar, olive oil, salt, and pepper.
3. Reserve a portion of the chimichurri sauce for serving and marinate the beef short ribs in the remaining sauce for at least 1-2 hours, or preferably overnight in the refrigerator.
4. Preheat the grill to medium-high heat.
5. Remove the beef from the marinade and grill for about 15-20 minutes, turning occasionally, or until the meat reaches your desired level of doneness.
6. Baste the ribs with the reserved chimichurri sauce during the last few minutes of grilling.
7. Once cooked, let the meat rest for a few minutes before serving.
8. Serve Asado Paraguayo hot, accompanied by additional chimichurri sauce on the side.

Bori Bori (Cornmeal Dumpling Soup)

Servings: 4-6

Time: 1.5 hours

Ingredients:

- 1 cup cornmeal
- 1/2 cup all-purpose flour
- 1 egg
- 1/4 cup milk
- 1 teaspoon salt
- 1 pound chicken, cut into bite-sized pieces
- 1 onion, finely chopped
- 2 cloves garlic, minced
- 1 bell pepper, diced
- 1 tomato, diced
- 1 cup pumpkin, peeled and diced
- 1 tablespoon vegetable oil
- 8 cups chicken broth
- Salt and pepper to taste
- Fresh parsley, chopped (for garnish)

Directions:

1. In a bowl, combine cornmeal, all-purpose flour, egg, milk, and salt to form a thick, sticky dough.

2. With wet hands, shape the dough into small dumplings, about the size of a walnut. Set aside.

3. In a large pot, heat vegetable oil over medium heat. Sauté chopped onions and minced garlic until softened.

4. Add chicken pieces to the pot and cook until browned on all sides.

5. Stir in diced bell peppers, tomatoes, and pumpkin. Cook for an additional 5 minutes.

6. Pour in chicken broth and bring the mixture to a boil.

7. Gently drop the cornmeal dumplings into the boiling broth, ensuring they are evenly distributed.

8. Reduce heat to simmer and cook for about 20-25 minutes, or until the dumplings are cooked through and the chicken is tender.

9. Season the soup with salt and pepper to taste.

10. Garnish with chopped fresh parsley before serving.

Caldo de Pescado (Fish Soup)

Servings: 4-6

Time: 1.5 hours

Ingredients:

- 1 pound white fish fillets, cut into chunks
- 1 onion, finely chopped
- 2 cloves garlic, minced
- 1 bell pepper, diced
- 2 tomatoes, diced
- 1 carrot, peeled and sliced
- 1 potato, peeled and diced
- 1/2 cup green peas
- 1/4 cup fresh cilantro, chopped
- 1 teaspoon ground cumin
- 1 bay leaf
- 8 cups fish or vegetable broth
- Salt and pepper to taste
- Lime wedges (for serving)

Directions:

1. In a large pot, sauté chopped onions and minced garlic until translucent.

2. Add diced bell peppers, tomatoes, carrots, and potatoes to the pot. Cook for 5-7 minutes until the vegetables begin to soften.

3. Pour in fish or vegetable broth and bring the mixture to a boil.

4. Reduce heat to simmer and add the white fish chunks, green peas, fresh cilantro, ground cumin, and a bay leaf.

5. Simmer for about 20-30 minutes or until the fish is cooked through and the vegetables are tender.

6. Season the soup with salt and pepper to taste.

7. Remove the bay leaf before serving.

8. Serve Caldo de Pescado hot, with lime wedges on the side for squeezing.

So'o Ku'i (Paraguayan Beef Stew)

Servings: 4-6

Time: 2 hours

Ingredients:

- 1.5 pounds beef stew meat, cubed
- 1 onion, finely chopped
- 2 cloves garlic, minced
- 1 bell pepper, diced
- 2 tomatoes, diced
- 1 cup pumpkin, peeled and diced
- 1 cup sweet potatoes, peeled and diced
- 1 cup corn kernels (fresh or frozen)
- 2 tablespoons vegetable oil
- 1 tablespoon tomato paste
- 1 teaspoon ground cumin
- 1 teaspoon paprika
- 1 bay leaf
- 4 cups beef broth
- Salt and pepper to taste
- Fresh parsley, chopped (for garnish)

Directions:

1. In a large pot, heat vegetable oil over medium heat. Sauté chopped onions and minced garlic until softened.

2. Add beef stew meat to the pot and brown on all sides.

3. Stir in diced bell peppers, tomatoes, pumpkin, sweet potatoes, and corn kernels. Cook for an additional 5 minutes.

4. Add tomato paste, ground cumin, paprika, and a bay leaf. Mix well.

5. Pour in beef broth and bring the mixture to a boil.

6. Reduce heat to simmer and cook for about 1.5 to 2 hours or until the meat is tender and the vegetables are cooked.

7. Season the stew with salt and pepper to taste.

8. Remove the bay leaf before serving.

9. Garnish with chopped fresh parsley and serve So'o Ku'i hot.

Yuca Rellena (Stuffed Cassava)

Servings: 4-6

Time: 1.5 hours

Ingredients:

- 2 pounds cassava (yuca), peeled and cut into chunks
- 1 pound ground beef
- 1 onion, finely chopped
- 2 cloves garlic, minced
- 1 bell pepper, diced
- 2 tomatoes, diced
- 1/2 cup green olives, pitted and sliced
- 1/2 cup raisins
- 1 teaspoon ground cumin
- 1 teaspoon paprika
- Salt and pepper to taste
- 2 tablespoons vegetable oil
- 1 cup tomato sauce
- 1 cup mozzarella cheese, shredded
- Fresh cilantro, chopped (for garnish)

Directions:

1. Boil the cassava chunks in a large pot of salted water until fork-tender, about 20-30 minutes. Drain and set aside.
2. Preheat the oven to 375°F (190°C).
3. In a skillet, heat vegetable oil over medium heat. Sauté chopped onions and minced garlic until translucent.
4. Add ground beef to the skillet and cook until browned. Stir in diced bell peppers, tomatoes, green olives, raisins, ground cumin, paprika, salt, and pepper. Cook for an additional 5 minutes.
5. Cut each cassava chunk in half lengthwise and remove the fibrous core.
6. Spoon the beef mixture onto the flat side of each cassava piece and roll them into stuffed rolls.
7. Place the stuffed cassava in a baking dish.
8. Pour tomato sauce over the stuffed cassava rolls and sprinkle with shredded mozzarella cheese.
9. Bake in the preheated oven for 20-25 minutes, or until the cheese is melted and bubbly.
10. Garnish with chopped fresh cilantro before serving.

Pira Caldo (Fish and Vegetable Stew)

Servings: 4-6

Time: 1.5 hours

Ingredients:

- 1 pound white fish fillets, cut into chunks
- 1 onion, finely chopped
- 2 cloves garlic, minced
- 1 bell pepper, diced
- 2 tomatoes, diced
- 1 carrot, peeled and sliced
- 1 zucchini, diced
- 1 cup green beans, trimmed and cut into bite-sized pieces
- 1 cup pumpkin, peeled and diced
- 2 tablespoons vegetable oil
- 1 teaspoon ground cumin
- 1 teaspoon paprika
- 1 bay leaf
- 6 cups fish or vegetable broth
- Salt and pepper to taste
- Fresh parsley, chopped (for garnish)

Directions:

1. In a large pot, heat vegetable oil over medium heat. Sauté chopped onions and minced garlic until translucent.

2. Add diced bell peppers, tomatoes, carrots, zucchini, green beans, and pumpkin to the pot. Cook for 5-7 minutes until the vegetables begin to soften.

3. Pour in fish or vegetable broth and bring the mixture to a boil.

4. Reduce heat to simmer and add white fish chunks, ground cumin, paprika, and a bay leaf.

5. Simmer for about 20-30 minutes or until the fish is cooked through and the vegetables are tender.

6. Season the stew with salt and pepper to taste.

7. Remove the bay leaf before serving.

8. Garnish with chopped fresh parsley and serve Pira Caldo hot.

Pastel de Masa (Corn and Meat Pie)

Servings: 6-8

Time: 2 hours

Ingredients:

- 2 cups cornmeal
- 2 cups hot water
- 1/2 cup lard or vegetable shortening
- 1 teaspoon salt
- 1 pound ground beef
- 1 onion, finely chopped
- 2 cloves garlic, minced
- 1 bell pepper, diced
- 2 tomatoes, diced
- 1/2 cup green olives, pitted and sliced
- 1 teaspoon ground cumin
- 1 teaspoon paprika
- Salt and pepper to taste
- 2 hard-boiled eggs, sliced
- 1/4 cup raisins (optional)
- 1 egg (for egg wash)

Directions:

1. In a large bowl, combine cornmeal, hot water, lard (or vegetable shortening), and salt. Mix until a soft dough forms. Let it rest while preparing the filling.

2. Preheat the oven to 375°F (190°C).

3. In a skillet, heat lard or oil over medium heat. Sauté chopped onions and minced garlic until translucent.

4. Add ground beef to the skillet and cook until browned. Stir in diced bell peppers, tomatoes, green olives, ground cumin, paprika, salt, and pepper. Cook for an additional 5 minutes.

5. Roll out half of the cornmeal dough on a floured surface to fit the bottom of a greased baking dish.

6. Place the rolled-out dough in the baking dish and press it to the edges.

7. Spoon the meat mixture over the dough in an even layer. Add sliced hard-boiled eggs and raisins if desired.

8. Roll out the remaining cornmeal dough to cover the meat filling. Seal the edges by pressing with a fork.

9. Beat an egg and brush it over the top crust for a golden finish.

10. Bake in the preheated oven for 30-40 minutes or until the crust is golden brown.

11. Allow Pastel de Masa to cool slightly before slicing.

Chipa Guasu (Corn and Cheese Casserole)

Servings: 8-10

Time: 1.5 hours

Ingredients:

- 4 cups fresh corn kernels (about 6-8 ears of corn)
- 1 cup cornmeal
- 1 cup milk
- 1/2 cup butter, melted
- 4 eggs
- 2 cups Paraguayan cheese (Queso Paraguay), grated
- 1 cup feta cheese, crumbled
- 1 onion, finely chopped
- 1 bell pepper, diced
- 1 teaspoon baking powder
- Salt to taste

Directions:

1. Preheat the oven to 375°F (190°C). Grease a baking dish.
2. In a blender, blend 2 cups of fresh corn kernels with milk until smooth. Set aside.
3. In a large mixing bowl, combine cornmeal, melted butter, and the blended corn mixture. Mix well.

4. Add eggs one at a time, incorporating each before adding the next.

5. Fold in the remaining 2 cups of corn kernels, grated Paraguayan cheese, crumbled feta cheese, chopped onions, diced bell peppers, baking powder, and salt.

6. Pour the mixture into the greased baking dish.

7. Bake for 45-55 minutes or until the top is golden brown and a toothpick inserted into the center comes out clean.

8. Allow Chipa Guasu to cool slightly before slicing.

Mbeju Rejao (Cheesy Cassava Cake)

Servings: 6-8

Time: 1.5 hours

Ingredients:

- 2 cups cassava (yuca), peeled and grated
- 1 cup cornstarch
- 1 cup whole milk
- 1/2 cup butter, melted
- 2 eggs
- 2 cups Paraguayan cheese (Queso Paraguay), grated
- 1 teaspoon salt

Directions:

1. Preheat the oven to 375°F (190°C). Grease a baking dish.
2. In a large bowl, combine grated cassava, cornstarch, and salt.
3. In a saucepan, heat the milk until warm. Add the melted butter to the warm milk and mix well.
4. Pour the milk and butter mixture over the cassava mixture. Stir until combined.
5. Beat the eggs and add them to the batter, mixing until smooth.

6. Fold in the grated Paraguayan cheese, ensuring an even distribution throughout the batter.

7. Pour the batter into the greased baking dish.

8. Bake for 45-55 minutes or until the top is golden brown and a toothpick inserted into the center comes out clean.

9. Allow Mbeju Rejao to cool slightly before slicing.

Vori Vori (Cheese and Cornmeal Dumplings)

Servings: 4-6

Time: 1 hour

Ingredients:

- 1 cup cornmeal
- 1/2 cup all-purpose flour
- 1 cup Paraguayan cheese (Queso Paraguay), grated
- 1/4 cup lard or vegetable shortening
- 1 egg
- 1/4 cup milk
- 1 teaspoon salt
- 6 cups chicken or vegetable broth

Directions:

1. In a large mixing bowl, combine cornmeal, all-purpose flour, and salt.
2. Add grated Paraguayan cheese to the dry ingredients and mix well.
3. In a small saucepan, melt lard or vegetable shortening. Allow it to cool slightly.
4. In a separate bowl, whisk together the egg, milk, and melted lard.

5. Pour the wet ingredients into the dry ingredients, stirring until a thick, sticky dough forms.

6. With wet hands, shape the dough into small dumplings, about the size of a walnut.

7. In a large pot, bring chicken or vegetable broth to a gentle boil.

8. Drop the dumplings into the boiling broth, allowing them to cook for about 15-20 minutes or until they float to the surface.

9. Once the dumplings are cooked through, serve Vori Vori hot in bowls with some of the broth.

SIDE DISHES

Mbeju de Harina (Flour and Cheese Pancake)

Servings: 4-6

Time: 45 minutes

Ingredients:

- 2 cups all-purpose flour
- 1 cup Paraguayan cheese (Queso Paraguay), grated
- 1/2 cup butter, melted
- 1/4 cup milk
- 1 egg
- 1/2 teaspoon salt

Directions:

1. Preheat a non-stick skillet or griddle over medium heat.

2. In a large mixing bowl, combine all-purpose flour, grated Paraguayan cheese, and salt.

3. In a separate bowl, whisk together melted butter, milk, and the egg.

4. Pour the wet ingredients into the dry ingredients, stirring until a thick batter forms.

5. Using a ladle, pour a portion of the batter onto the preheated skillet, spreading it thinly to form a pancake.

6. Cook until the edges are golden brown, then flip and cook the other side until done.

7. Repeat the process with the remaining batter.

Sopa Paraguaya de Carne (Meat Cornbread)

Servings: 6-8

Time: 1.5 hours

Ingredients:

- 2 cups cornmeal
- 2 cups whole milk
- 1/2 cup vegetable oil
- 1 onion, finely chopped
- 1 bell pepper, diced
- 2 tomatoes, diced
- 1 pound beef stew meat, cubed
- 2 eggs
- 1 cup Paraguayan cheese (Queso Paraguay), grated
- 1 tablespoon baking powder
- Salt and pepper to taste

Directions:

1. Preheat the oven to 375°F (190°C). Grease a baking dish.
2. In a bowl, combine cornmeal and whole milk. Let it rest for 10 minutes.
3. In a skillet, heat vegetable oil over medium heat. Sauté chopped onions, diced bell peppers, and tomatoes until softened.

4. Add beef stew meat to the skillet and cook until browned. Season with salt and pepper.

5. In a large mixing bowl, beat the eggs and add them to the cornmeal mixture. Mix well.

6. Add the sautéed vegetables and beef to the cornmeal mixture. Stir in grated Paraguayan cheese and baking powder. Mix until well combined.

7. Pour the batter into the greased baking dish.

8. Bake for 40-50 minutes or until the top is golden brown and a toothpick inserted into the center comes out clean.

9. Allow Sopa Paraguaya de Carne to cool slightly before slicing.

Quibebe (Pumpkin Stew)

Servings: 4-6

Time: 1 hour

Ingredients:

- 1 pound beef stew meat, cubed
- 1 onion, finely chopped
- 2 cloves garlic, minced
- 1 bell pepper, diced
- 2 tomatoes, diced
- 1 pumpkin, peeled and diced (about 4 cups)
- 1 cup corn kernels (fresh or frozen)
- 2 tablespoons vegetable oil
- 1 teaspoon ground cumin
- 1 teaspoon paprika
- Salt and pepper to taste
- Fresh parsley, chopped (for garnish)

Directions:

1. In a large pot, heat vegetable oil over medium heat. Sauté chopped onions and minced garlic until translucent.
2. Add beef stew meat to the pot and brown on all sides.
3. Stir in diced bell peppers and tomatoes. Cook for an additional 5 minutes.

4. Add diced pumpkin and corn kernels to the pot. Mix well.

5. Season with ground cumin, paprika, salt, and pepper. Stir to coat the ingredients evenly.

6. Pour in enough water to cover the ingredients and bring the stew to a boil.

7. Reduce heat to simmer and cook for about 30-40 minutes or until the meat is tender and the pumpkin is cooked through.

8. Adjust seasoning to taste.

9. Garnish with chopped fresh parsley before serving.

Pajagua Mascada (Mashed Pumpkin)

Servings: 4-6

Time: 45 minutes

Ingredients:

- 1 pumpkin, peeled and diced (about 4 cups)
- 2 tablespoons butter
- 1/4 cup milk
- Salt and pepper to taste
- Fresh parsley, chopped (for garnish)

Directions:

1. Place diced pumpkin in a pot and cover with water. Bring to a boil and cook until the pumpkin is fork-tender, about 20-25 minutes.
2. Drain the cooked pumpkin and return it to the pot.
3. Mash the pumpkin using a potato masher or fork until smooth.
4. In a small saucepan, melt butter over low heat.
5. Add the melted butter and milk to the mashed pumpkin. Continue to mash and stir until well combined.
6. Season with salt and pepper to taste. Adjust the seasoning as needed.

7. Cook the mashed pumpkin over low heat for an additional 5-10 minutes, allowing the flavors to meld.

8. Garnish with chopped fresh parsley before serving.

Locro (Vegetable and Meat Stew)

Servings: 6-8

Time: 2 hours

Ingredients:

- 1 pound beef stew meat, cubed
- 1 onion, finely chopped
- 2 cloves garlic, minced
- 1 bell pepper, diced
- 2 tomatoes, diced
- 1 cup corn kernels (fresh or frozen)
- 1 cup white hominy (mote)
- 1 cup pumpkin, peeled and diced
- 2 potatoes, peeled and diced
- 1/2 cup green beans, trimmed and cut into bite-sized pieces
- 2 tablespoons vegetable oil
- 1 teaspoon ground cumin
- 1 teaspoon paprika
- Salt and pepper to taste
- Fresh parsley, chopped (for garnish)

Directions:

1. In a large pot, heat vegetable oil over medium heat. Sauté chopped onions and minced garlic until translucent.

2. Add beef stew meat to the pot and brown on all sides.

3. Stir in diced bell peppers and tomatoes. Cook for an additional 5 minutes.

4. Add white hominy, diced pumpkin, potatoes, green beans, and corn kernels to the pot. Mix well.

5. Pour in enough water to cover the ingredients and bring the stew to a boil.

6. Reduce heat to simmer and add ground cumin, paprika, salt, and pepper. Stir to combine.

7. Cook for about 1.5 to 2 hours or until the meat is tender and the vegetables are cooked.

8. Adjust seasoning to taste.

9. Garnish with chopped fresh parsley before serving.

Chipa So'o (Paraguayan Cornbread)

Servings: 8-10

Time: 1.5 hours

Ingredients:

- 2 cups cornmeal
- 1 cup all-purpose flour
- 1 cup Paraguayan cheese (Queso Paraguay), grated
- 1/2 cup butter, melted
- 1/4 cup milk
- 3 eggs
- 1 teaspoon baking powder
- 1/2 teaspoon salt

Directions:

1. Preheat the oven to 375°F (190°C). Grease a baking dish.
2. In a large mixing bowl, combine cornmeal, all-purpose flour, grated Paraguayan cheese, baking powder, and salt.
3. In a separate bowl, whisk together melted butter, milk, and eggs.
4. Pour the wet ingredients into the dry ingredients, stirring until a thick batter forms.
5. Transfer the batter into the greased baking dish.

6. Bake for 35-45 minutes or until the top is golden brown and a toothpick inserted into the center comes out clean.

7. Allow Chipa So'o to cool slightly before slicing.

Lentejas con Yuca (Lentils with Cassava)

Servings: 4-6

Time: 1.5 hours

Ingredients:

- 1 cup dried lentils, rinsed
- 1 yuca (cassava), peeled and diced
- 1 onion, finely chopped
- 2 cloves garlic, minced
- 1 bell pepper, diced
- 2 tomatoes, diced
- 1 carrot, peeled and sliced
- 2 tablespoons vegetable oil
- 1 teaspoon ground cumin
- 1 teaspoon paprika
- 1 bay leaf
- 6 cups vegetable or chicken broth
- Salt and pepper to taste
- Fresh cilantro, chopped (for garnish)

Directions:

1. In a large pot, heat vegetable oil over medium heat. Sauté chopped onions and minced garlic until translucent.

2. Add diced bell peppers, tomatoes, carrots, and yuca to the pot. Cook for 5-7 minutes until the vegetables begin to soften.

3. Pour in vegetable or chicken broth and bring the mixture to a boil.

4. Add rinsed lentils, ground cumin, paprika, and a bay leaf. Mix well.

5. Reduce heat to simmer and cook for about 45-60 minutes or until the lentils are tender and the yuca is cooked through.

6. Season the stew with salt and pepper to taste.

7. Remove the bay leaf before serving.

8. Garnish with chopped fresh cilantro and serve Lentejas con Yuca hot.

Pudín de Pan (Bread Pudding)

Servings: 6-8

Time: 1.5 hours

Ingredients:

- 6 cups stale bread, torn into small pieces
- 2 cups whole milk
- 3/4 cup sugar
- 3 eggs
- 1/4 cup butter, melted
- 1 teaspoon vanilla extract
- 1/2 cup raisins (optional)
- Ground cinnamon (for sprinkling)

Directions:

1. Preheat the oven to 350°F (175°C). Grease a baking dish.
2. In a large mixing bowl, soak the torn bread pieces in whole milk for about 10-15 minutes.
3. In a separate bowl, beat eggs and sugar together until well combined.
4. Add the melted butter and vanilla extract to the egg mixture. Mix thoroughly.
5. Pour the egg mixture over the soaked bread, stirring to ensure the bread is well coated.

6. Fold in raisins if desired.

7. Transfer the mixture to the greased baking dish, spreading it evenly.

8. Sprinkle ground cinnamon over the top of the pudding.

9. Bake for 45-60 minutes or until the top is golden brown and a toothpick inserted into the center comes out clean.

10. Allow Pudín de Pan to cool slightly before serving.

11. Serve warm, either on its own or with a dollop of whipped cream or a scoop of vanilla ice cream.

Pira Pytã (Grilled Fish)

Servings: 4

Time: 30 minutes

Ingredients:

- 4 whole fish (such as tilapia or catfish), cleaned and scaled
- 1/4 cup vegetable oil
- 2 tablespoons lemon juice
- 2 cloves garlic, minced
- 1 teaspoon ground cumin
- 1 teaspoon paprika
- Salt and pepper to taste
- Fresh parsley, chopped (for garnish)
- Lemon wedges (for serving)

Directions:

1. Preheat the grill to medium-high heat.
2. In a small bowl, mix vegetable oil, lemon juice, minced garlic, ground cumin, paprika, salt, and pepper to create a marinade.
3. Make diagonal cuts on both sides of each fish, allowing the marinade to penetrate.

4. Brush the fish generously with the prepared marinade, ensuring it reaches the cuts.

5. Place the fish on the preheated grill and cook for about 15-20 minutes, turning once halfway through, or until the fish is cooked through and has a nice grilled char.

6. Baste the fish with the remaining marinade during grilling for added flavor.

7. Garnish with chopped fresh parsley before serving.

8. Serve Pira Pytã hot off the grill, accompanied by lemon wedges for a burst of citrus freshness.

Vatapá Paraguayo (Paraguayan Fish Stew)

Servings: 4-6

Time: 1.5 hours

Ingredients:

- 1 pound white fish fillets, cut into chunks
- 1 onion, finely chopped
- 2 cloves garlic, minced
- 1 bell pepper, diced
- 2 tomatoes, diced
- 1 cup pumpkin, peeled and diced
- 1 cup coconut milk
- 1 cup fish or vegetable broth
- 2 tablespoons vegetable oil
- 1/2 cup peanuts, finely ground
- 1/4 cup cornstarch
- 1 teaspoon ground cumin
- 1 teaspoon paprika
- Salt and pepper to taste
- Fresh cilantro, chopped (for garnish)
- Lime wedges (for serving)

Directions:

1. In a large pot, heat vegetable oil over medium heat. Sauté chopped onions and minced garlic until translucent.

2. Add diced bell peppers, tomatoes, and pumpkin to the pot. Cook for 5-7 minutes until the vegetables begin to soften.

3. Pour in fish or vegetable broth and coconut milk. Mix well.

4. In a small bowl, combine ground peanuts, cornstarch, ground cumin, paprika, salt, and pepper to create a paste.

5. Add the peanut paste to the pot, stirring continuously to avoid lumps.

6. Bring the stew to a gentle boil, then reduce heat to simmer.

7. Add white fish chunks to the pot and simmer for about 20-30 minutes or until the fish is cooked through.

8. Adjust seasoning to taste.

9. Garnish with chopped fresh cilantro before serving.

10. Serve Vatapá Paraguayo hot, accompanied by lime wedges for a zesty finish.

SNACKS

Mandi'o Chyryry (Cassava Croquettes)

Servings: 4-6

Time: 1.5 hours

Ingredients:

- 2 cups cassava (yuca), peeled and grated
- 1/2 cup cornmeal
- 1/4 cup all-purpose flour
- 1/2 cup Paraguayan cheese (Queso Paraguay), grated
- 2 eggs
- 2 tablespoons fresh parsley, finely chopped
- 2 cloves garlic, minced
- Salt and pepper to taste

- Vegetable oil for frying

Directions:

1. In a large mixing bowl, combine grated cassava, cornmeal, all-purpose flour, grated Paraguayan cheese, chopped fresh parsley, minced garlic, salt, and pepper.
2. Beat the eggs and add them to the mixture, stirring until a thick dough forms.
3. With wet hands, shape the dough into small croquettes or patties.
4. In a skillet, heat vegetable oil over medium heat.
5. Fry the cassava croquettes until golden brown on both sides, ensuring they are cooked through.
6. Remove from the skillet and place on paper towels to absorb excess oil.

Sopa de Poroto (Bean Soup)

Servings: 6-8

Time: 1.5 hours

Ingredients:

- 2 cups dried white beans, soaked overnight
- 1 onion, finely chopped
- 2 cloves garlic, minced
- 2 carrots, peeled and sliced
- 2 potatoes, peeled and diced
- 1/2 cup celery, chopped
- 1 bay leaf
- 2 tablespoons vegetable oil
- 6 cups vegetable or chicken broth
- Salt and pepper to taste
- Fresh parsley, chopped (for garnish)

Directions:

1. In a large pot, heat vegetable oil over medium heat. Sauté chopped onions and minced garlic until translucent.
2. Add soaked and drained white beans to the pot. Cook for a few minutes, stirring occasionally.
3. Pour in vegetable or chicken broth, ensuring it covers the beans.

4. Add sliced carrots, diced potatoes, chopped celery, and a bay leaf to the pot. Mix well.

5. Bring the soup to a boil, then reduce heat to simmer.

6. Cook for about 1 to 1.5 hours or until the beans are tender and the vegetables are cooked through.

7. Season with salt and pepper to taste.

8. Remove the bay leaf before serving.

9. Garnish with chopped fresh parsley.

Yuca Frita (Fried Cassava)

Servings: 4-6

Time: 45 minutes

Ingredients:

- 2 large yucas (cassava), peeled and cut into thick strips
- Vegetable oil for frying
- Salt to taste

Directions:

1. Peel the yucas and cut them into thick strips, similar to French fries.
2. In a large pot or deep fryer, heat vegetable oil to 350°F (175°C).
3. Carefully place the yuca strips into the hot oil, ensuring not to overcrowd the pot.
4. Fry the yuca strips until they are golden brown and crispy, approximately 8-10 minutes.
5. Use a slotted spoon to remove the fried yuca from the oil and place them on paper towels to absorb excess oil.
6. While still hot, sprinkle the fried yuca with salt to taste.

Chipa Guasu de Lata (Canned Corn and Cheese Casserole)

Servings: 8-10

Time: 1 hour

Ingredients:

- 1 can (about 15 ounces) whole kernel corn, drained
- 1 can (about 15 ounces) creamed corn
- 1 cup all-purpose flour
- 1 cup Paraguayan cheese (Queso Paraguay), grated
- 1/2 cup butter, melted
- 3 eggs
- 1 teaspoon baking powder
- 1/2 teaspoon salt
- Fresh parsley, chopped (for garnish)

Directions:

1. Preheat the oven to 375°F (190°C). Grease a baking dish.
2. In a large mixing bowl, combine drained whole kernel corn, creamed corn, all-purpose flour, grated Paraguayan cheese, melted butter, eggs, baking powder, and salt.
3. Mix the ingredients thoroughly until a consistent batter is formed.
4. Pour the batter into the greased baking dish.

5. Bake for 45-50 minutes or until the top is golden brown and a toothpick inserted into the center comes out clean.

6. Allow Chipa Guasu de Lata to cool slightly before slicing.

7. Garnish with chopped fresh parsley for a vibrant touch.

Sopa de Lentejas (Lentil Soup)

Servings: 6-8

Time: 1.5 hours

Ingredients:

- 1 cup dried lentils, rinsed
- 1 onion, finely chopped
- 2 carrots, peeled and sliced
- 2 potatoes, peeled and diced
- 2 cloves garlic, minced
- 2 tablespoons vegetable oil
- 6 cups vegetable or chicken broth
- 1 teaspoon ground cumin
- 1 teaspoon paprika
- 1 bay leaf
- Salt and pepper to taste
- Fresh cilantro, chopped (for garnish)
- Lemon wedges (for serving)

Directions:

1. In a large pot, heat vegetable oil over medium heat. Sauté chopped onions and minced garlic until translucent.
2. Add rinsed lentils to the pot and stir for a few minutes.

3. Pour in vegetable or chicken broth, ensuring it covers the lentils.

4. Add sliced carrots, diced potatoes, ground cumin, paprika, and a bay leaf to the pot. Mix well.

5. Bring the soup to a boil, then reduce heat to simmer.

6. Cook for about 1 to 1.5 hours or until the lentils are tender and the vegetables are cooked through.

7. Season with salt and pepper to taste.

8. Remove the bay leaf before serving.

9. Garnish with chopped fresh cilantro.

10. Serve Sopa de Lentejas hot, accompanied by lemon wedges for a zesty touch.

Pan Casero (Homemade Bread)

Servings: 1 loaf

Time: 3 hours (including rising time)

Ingredients:

- 4 cups all-purpose flour
- 2 teaspoons active dry yeast
- 1 tablespoon sugar
- 1 1/2 teaspoons salt
- 1 1/4 cups warm water (110°F/43°C)
- 2 tablespoons olive oil

Directions:

1. In a small bowl, combine warm water, sugar, and active dry yeast. Let it sit for about 5-10 minutes, or until the mixture becomes frothy.
2. In a large mixing bowl, combine the flour and salt.
3. Create a well in the center of the flour mixture and pour in the activated yeast mixture and olive oil.
4. Stir the ingredients together until a dough forms.
5. On a floured surface, knead the dough for about 8-10 minutes, or until it becomes smooth and elastic.

6. Place the dough in a lightly oiled bowl, cover it with a clean kitchen towel, and let it rise in a warm place for 1-1.5 hours, or until it doubles in size.

7. Preheat the oven to 375°F (190°C).

8. Punch down the risen dough and shape it into a loaf. Place the shaped dough in a greased loaf pan.

9. Allow the dough to rise for an additional 30-45 minutes.

10. Bake the bread in the preheated oven for 25-30 minutes, or until the top is golden brown and the bread sounds hollow when tapped.

11. Remove the bread from the oven and let it cool in the pan for 10 minutes before transferring it to a wire rack to cool completely.

12. Slice and serve Pan Casero as a delightful addition to your meals or enjoy it with your favorite spreads.

Empanadas de Carne (Meat Empanadas)

Servings: 12

Time: 2 hours

Ingredients: *For the Dough:*

- 3 cups all-purpose flour
- 1 cup unsalted butter, cold and cut into small pieces
- 1 teaspoon salt
- 1/2 cup cold water

For the Filling:

- 1 pound ground beef
- 1 onion, finely chopped
- 2 hard-boiled eggs, chopped
- 1/2 cup green olives, pitted and sliced
- 1/4 cup raisins
- 2 tablespoons vegetable oil
- 1 teaspoon ground cumin
- 1 teaspoon paprika
- Salt and pepper to taste

Directions: *For the Dough:*

1. In a large bowl, combine flour and salt. Add the cold butter pieces and mix until the mixture resembles coarse crumbs.

2. Gradually add cold water, mixing until the dough comes together. Form it into a ball, wrap in plastic wrap, and refrigerate for at least 30 minutes.

For the Filling:

1. In a skillet, heat vegetable oil over medium heat. Sauté chopped onions until translucent.

2. Add ground beef to the skillet and cook until browned. Drain excess fat.

3. Stir in ground cumin, paprika, salt, and pepper. Mix well.

4. Add chopped hard-boiled eggs, sliced olives, and raisins to the beef mixture. Cook for an additional 2-3 minutes. Remove from heat and let it cool.

Assembly:

1. Preheat the oven to 375°F (190°C).

2. On a floured surface, roll out the chilled dough to about 1/8-inch thickness.

3. Using a round cutter or a bowl, cut out circles from the dough.

4. Place a spoonful of the meat filling in the center of each dough circle.

5. Fold the dough over the filling, creating a half-moon shape. Seal the edges by pressing with a fork.

6. Place the empanadas on a baking sheet and bake for 20-25 minutes or until golden brown.

7. Allow Empanadas de Carne to cool slightly before serving.

Tortilla Paraguaya (Paraguayan Omelette)

Servings: 4-6

Time: 30 minutes

Ingredients:

- 2 cups cornmeal
- 1 cup all-purpose flour
- 1 cup Paraguayan cheese (Queso Paraguay), grated
- 1 onion, finely chopped
- 2 cups milk
- 4 eggs
- 1/4 cup vegetable oil
- Salt and pepper to taste

Directions:

1. In a large mixing bowl, combine cornmeal, all-purpose flour, grated Paraguayan cheese, and chopped onions.
2. In a separate bowl, whisk together eggs and milk until well combined.
3. Pour the egg and milk mixture into the dry ingredients, stirring until a smooth batter forms.
4. Season the batter with salt and pepper to taste. Mix well.
5. In a large skillet, heat vegetable oil over medium heat.

6. Pour the batter into the skillet, spreading it evenly to cover the bottom.

7. Cook for 10-15 minutes or until the edges are set and the bottom is golden brown.

8. Carefully flip the omelette using a large plate or by sliding it onto a flat surface and then returning it to the skillet to cook the other side.

9. Cook for an additional 10-15 minutes or until the omelette is cooked through and golden brown on both sides.

10. Remove from the skillet and let it cool slightly before slicing.

Pastel de Mandioca (Cassava Pie)

Servings: 6-8

Time: 2 hours

Ingredients: *For the Dough:*

- 4 cups cassava (yuca), peeled and grated
- 1 cup all-purpose flour
- 1/2 cup butter, softened
- 2 eggs
- Salt to taste

For the Filling:

- 1 pound ground beef
- 1 onion, finely chopped
- 2 tomatoes, diced
- 1 bell pepper, diced
- 2 hard-boiled eggs, sliced
- 1/2 cup green olives, pitted and sliced
- 2 tablespoons vegetable oil
- 1 teaspoon ground cumin
- 1 teaspoon paprika
- Salt and pepper to taste

Directions: *For the Dough:*

1. In a large mixing bowl, combine grated cassava, all-purpose flour, softened butter, eggs, and salt. Mix until a soft dough forms.
2. Divide the dough into two portions - one for the bottom crust and one for the top crust.

For the Filling:

1. In a skillet, heat vegetable oil over medium heat. Sauté chopped onions until translucent.
2. Add ground beef to the skillet and cook until browned. Drain excess fat.
3. Stir in diced tomatoes, diced bell peppers, ground cumin, paprika, salt, and pepper. Mix well.
4. Add sliced hard-boiled eggs and sliced olives to the beef mixture. Cook for an additional 2-3 minutes. Remove from heat and let it cool.

Assembly:

1. Preheat the oven to 375°F (190°C).
2. Roll out one portion of the cassava dough and line the bottom of a greased pie dish.
3. Spoon the cooled beef filling over the bottom crust.
4. Roll out the second portion of the cassava dough and place it over the filling, sealing the edges.
5. Bake for 30-40 minutes or until the top is golden brown.

6. Allow Pastel de Mandioca to cool slightly before slicing.

Mbaipy So'o (Paraguayan Corn Soup)

Servings: 6-8

Time: 1.5 hours

Ingredients:

- 2 cups fresh or frozen corn kernels
- 1 onion, finely chopped
- 2 cloves garlic, minced
- 1 bell pepper, diced
- 2 tomatoes, diced
- 1 carrot, peeled and sliced
- 2 potatoes, peeled and diced
- 2 tablespoons vegetable oil
- 6 cups chicken or vegetable broth
- 1 cup milk
- 1/4 cup fresh parsley, chopped
- Salt and pepper to taste
- Hard-boiled eggs, sliced (for garnish)

Directions:

1. In a large pot, heat vegetable oil over medium heat. Sauté chopped onions and minced garlic until translucent.

2. Add diced bell peppers, diced tomatoes, sliced carrots, and diced potatoes to the pot. Cook for 5-7 minutes until the vegetables begin to soften.

3. Pour in chicken or vegetable broth, ensuring it covers the vegetables.

4. Add fresh or frozen corn kernels to the pot. Mix well.

5. Bring the soup to a boil, then reduce heat to simmer.

6. Cook for about 45-60 minutes or until the vegetables are tender.

7. Stir in milk and fresh parsley, allowing the soup to simmer for an additional 10 minutes.

8. Season with salt and pepper to taste.

9. Remove from heat and let the soup cool slightly before serving.

10. Garnish each bowl of Mbaipy So'o with sliced hard-boiled eggs.

DESSERTS

Dulce de Mamón (Sweet Papaya)

Servings: Makes approximately 4 cups

Time: 2 hours

Ingredients:

- 1 large ripe papaya, peeled, seeded, and diced
- 2 cups granulated sugar
- 1 cinnamon stick
- 1/2 cup water
- Juice of 1 lime

Directions:

1. In a large saucepan, combine diced papaya, granulated sugar, cinnamon stick, and water.

2. Place the saucepan over medium heat, stirring until the sugar dissolves.

3. Bring the mixture to a boil, then reduce the heat to a simmer.

4. Cook for approximately 1.5 to 2 hours, stirring occasionally, or until the papaya is translucent and the syrup thickens.

5. Add the juice of 1 lime and stir to combine. Cook for an additional 5 minutes.

6. Remove the cinnamon stick and discard.

7. Let the Dulce de Mamón cool to room temperature before transferring it to sterilized jars.

8. Refrigerate for a few hours or overnight to allow the flavors to meld.

9. Serve on its own or as a topping for desserts, pancakes, or toast.

Queso y Miel (Cheese with Honey)

Servings: Varies based on preference

Time: 5 minutes

Ingredients:

- Assorted Paraguayan cheeses (Queso Paraguay or other local varieties)
- Honey (preferably a mild floral honey)

Directions:

1. Arrange the assorted Paraguayan cheeses on a serving platter.
2. Place a small bowl of honey alongside the cheese.
3. Serve the cheese with honey as a delightful pairing for a quick and elegant snack or appetizer.
4. Drizzle honey over the cheese just before eating.
5. Experiment with different cheese varieties and honeys to find your preferred flavor combination.

Mazamorra (Corn Pudding)

Servings: 6-8

Time: 1.5 hours

Ingredients:

- 1 cup yellow cornmeal
- 4 cups whole milk
- 1 cup granulated sugar
- 1 cinnamon stick
- 1 teaspoon vanilla extract
- Pinch of salt
- Cinnamon powder (for garnish)

Directions:

1. In a bowl, mix the cornmeal with a small amount of milk to create a smooth paste. Set aside.
2. In a large saucepan, combine the remaining milk, granulated sugar, and cinnamon stick.
3. Place the saucepan over medium heat and bring the mixture to a gentle boil, stirring to dissolve the sugar.
4. Gradually whisk in the cornmeal paste, stirring continuously to avoid lumps.

5. Reduce the heat to low and simmer, stirring frequently, until the mixture thickens to a pudding-like consistency. This may take about 45-60 minutes.

6. Stir in vanilla extract and a pinch of salt, continuing to cook for an additional 5 minutes.

7. Remove the cinnamon stick and discard.

8. Pour the Mazamorra into individual serving bowls or a large serving dish.

9. Allow it to cool to room temperature, then refrigerate for at least 1 hour before serving.

10. Sprinkle cinnamon powder over the Mazamorra just before serving.

Cocido (Boiled Fruit Dessert)

Servings: 6-8

Time: 1.5 hours

Ingredients:

- 4 cups water
- 1 cup peeled and diced sweet potatoes
- 1 cup peeled and diced pumpkin
- 1 cup peeled and diced apples
- 1 cup peeled and diced pears
- 1 cup peeled and diced quince
- 1 cup peeled and diced peaches
- 1 cup granulated sugar
- 1 cinnamon stick
- 1 tablespoon honey
- 1 cup cooked hominy or corn kernels (optional)
- Fresh mint leaves (for garnish)

Directions:

1. In a large pot, combine water, diced sweet potatoes, pumpkin, apples, pears, quince, and peaches.
2. Add granulated sugar and a cinnamon stick to the pot. Stir well.

3. Place the pot over medium heat and bring the mixture to a boil.

4. Reduce the heat to low and let the fruits simmer for about 1-1.5 hours, or until they are tender.

5. Add honey to the pot, stirring gently to incorporate the sweetness.

6. If desired, include cooked hominy or corn kernels to the mixture for an extra layer of texture.

7. Remove the cinnamon stick before serving.

8. Ladle the Cocido into serving bowls, ensuring a mix of fruits in each portion.

9. Garnish with fresh mint leaves for a burst of color and aroma.

Sopa de Gelatina (Fruit Jelly Soup)

Servings: 4-6

Time: 4 hours (including chilling time)

Ingredients:

- 1 package (3 ounces) fruit-flavored gelatin (choose a flavor of your preference)
- 2 cups boiling water
- 2 cups mixed fruits (such as diced peaches, strawberries, and canned fruit cocktail)
- 1/4 cup granulated sugar
- 1 tablespoon lemon juice
- 4 cups cold water
- Fresh mint leaves (for garnish)

Directions:

1. In a bowl, dissolve the fruit-flavored gelatin in 2 cups of boiling water, stirring until fully dissolved.
2. In a separate bowl, combine mixed fruits with granulated sugar and lemon juice. Let it sit for 10 minutes to allow the fruits to release their juices.
3. Add 4 cups of cold water to the dissolved gelatin mixture, stirring to combine.
4. Gently fold the mixed fruits into the gelatin mixture.

5. Pour the mixture into a glass or plastic serving bowl.

6. Refrigerate for at least 3-4 hours or until the gelatin is fully set.

7. Before serving, garnish with fresh mint leaves for a burst of freshness.

Pastel de Almidón (Starch Cake)

Servings: 8-10

Time: 2 hours

Ingredients: *For the Cake:*

- 2 cups cassava starch (almidón de mandioca)
- 1 cup granulated sugar
- 1 cup unsalted butter, softened
- 4 eggs
- 1 cup milk
- 1 teaspoon baking powder
- 1 teaspoon vanilla extract

For the Icing:

- 1 cup powdered sugar
- 2 tablespoons milk
- 1/2 teaspoon vanilla extract
- Coconut flakes (for garnish)

Directions: *For the Cake:*

1. Preheat the oven to 350°F (175°C). Grease and flour a round cake pan.
2. In a large mixing bowl, cream together softened butter and granulated sugar until light and fluffy.

3. Add eggs one at a time, beating well after each addition.

4. In a separate bowl, combine cassava starch and baking powder.

5. Gradually add the dry ingredients to the butter and sugar mixture, alternating with milk. Begin and end with the dry ingredients.

6. Stir in vanilla extract and mix until just combined.

7. Pour the batter into the prepared cake pan and smooth the top.

8. Bake for 45-50 minutes or until a toothpick inserted into the center comes out clean.

9. Allow the cake to cool completely before icing.

For the Icing:

1. In a small bowl, whisk together powdered sugar, milk, and vanilla extract until smooth.

2. Once the cake is cool, spread the icing evenly over the top.

3. Sprinkle coconut flakes on top of the icing for a decorative touch.

4. Allow the icing to set before slicing and serving.

Cocido con Leche (Milk Dessert)

Servings: 4-6

Time: 1 hour

Ingredients:

- 4 cups whole milk
- 1/2 cup sugar
- 1/2 cup rice, rinsed
- 1 cinnamon stick
- 1 teaspoon vanilla extract
- Ground cinnamon (for garnish)

Directions:

1. In a medium-sized saucepan, combine whole milk, sugar, and rinsed rice.
2. Add a cinnamon stick to the saucepan for flavor.
3. Place the saucepan over medium heat and bring the mixture to a gentle boil, stirring occasionally to prevent the rice from sticking to the bottom.
4. Once the mixture is boiling, reduce the heat to low and let it simmer for approximately 45 minutes to 1 hour, or until the rice is tender and the dessert has thickened.
5. Stir in vanilla extract, mixing well to incorporate the flavor.

6. Remove the cinnamon stick and discard.

7. Allow the Cocido con Leche to cool slightly before serving.

8. Ladle the dessert into individual bowls, and sprinkle ground cinnamon on top for an extra layer of flavor and a decorative touch.

Arroz con Leche (Rice Pudding)

Servings: 6-8

Time: 1.5 hours

Ingredients:

- 1 cup white rice
- 4 cups whole milk
- 1 cup sugar
- 1 cinnamon stick
- 1 teaspoon vanilla extract
- Ground cinnamon (for garnish)

Directions:

1. Rinse the white rice under cold water until the water runs clear.
2. In a medium-sized saucepan, combine rinsed rice, whole milk, sugar, and a cinnamon stick.
3. Place the saucepan over medium heat and bring the mixture to a boil, stirring occasionally.
4. Once the mixture is boiling, reduce the heat to low and let it simmer for approximately 1 to 1.5 hours, or until the rice is tender and the pudding has thickened to your desired consistency.
5. Stir in vanilla extract, mixing well to enhance the flavor.

6. Remove the cinnamon stick and discard.

7. Allow the Arroz con Leche to cool slightly before serving.

8. Ladle the rice pudding into individual bowls, and sprinkle ground cinnamon on top for an aromatic finish.

Rosquitas (Paraguayan Doughnuts)

Servings: 12-15 doughnuts

Time: 2 hours

Ingredients: *For the Dough:*

- 3 cups all-purpose flour
- 1/2 cup granulated sugar
- 1 teaspoon baking powder
- 1/2 teaspoon salt
- 2 tablespoons unsalted butter, melted
- 2 large eggs
- 1 cup whole milk
- Vegetable oil (for frying)

For the Coating:

- 1/2 cup granulated sugar
- 1 teaspoon ground cinnamon

Directions: *For the Dough:*

1. In a large mixing bowl, combine all-purpose flour, granulated sugar, baking powder, and salt.
2. In a separate bowl, whisk together melted butter, eggs, and whole milk.

3. Pour the wet ingredients into the dry ingredients, stirring until a soft dough forms.

4. Turn the dough onto a floured surface and knead gently for a few minutes until smooth.

5. Roll out the dough to about 1/2-inch thickness.

6. Use a round cutter to cut out doughnut shapes. You can use a smaller cutter to create a hole in the center.

7. Heat vegetable oil in a deep fryer or large, deep pan to 350°F (175°C).

8. Fry the doughnuts in batches until golden brown, turning once to ensure even cooking. This should take about 2-3 minutes per side.

9. Remove the doughnuts with a slotted spoon and drain on paper towels.

For the Coating:

1. In a bowl, combine granulated sugar and ground cinnamon.

2. While the doughnuts are still warm, roll them in the sugar and cinnamon mixture to coat evenly.

Dulce de Batata (Sweet Potato Jam)

Servings: Makes approximately 2 cups

Time: 1.5 hours

Ingredients:

- 2 cups sweet potatoes, peeled and diced
- 1 cup granulated sugar
- 1 cup water
- 1 cinnamon stick
- 1 teaspoon lemon zest
- Juice of 1 lemon

Directions:

1. In a medium-sized saucepan, combine diced sweet potatoes, granulated sugar, water, cinnamon stick, and lemon zest.
2. Place the saucepan over medium heat and bring the mixture to a boil.
3. Reduce the heat to low and let it simmer, stirring occasionally, for approximately 1 to 1.5 hours or until the sweet potatoes are tender and the mixture thickens into a jam-like consistency.
4. Add the juice of 1 lemon to the saucepan, stirring to incorporate the citrusy flavor.

5. Continue to simmer for an additional 10 minutes, allowing the jam to thicken further.

6. Remove the cinnamon stick and discard.

7. Let the Dulce de Batata cool to room temperature before transferring it to sterilized jars.

8. Refrigerate for a few hours or overnight to allow the flavors to meld.

9. Serve this homemade Sweet Potato Jam on toast, crackers, or as a delightful accompaniment to cheese.

MEASURES

1. **Volume Conversions:**
   - **1 cup = 240 milliliters**
   - **1 tablespoon = 15 milliliters**
   - **1 teaspoon = 5 milliliters**
   - **1 fluid ounce = 30 milliliters**
2. **Weight Conversions:**
   - **1 ounce = 28 grams**
   - **1 pound = 453 grams**
   - **1 kilogram = 2.2 pounds**
3. **Temperature Conversions:**
   - **Celsius to Fahrenheit: $F = (C \times 9/5) + 32$**
   - **Fahrenheit to Celsius: $C = (F - 32) \times 5/9$**
4. **Length Conversions:**
   - **1 inch = 2.54 centimeters**

- 1 foot = 30.48 centimeters
- 1 meter = 39.37 inches

5. **Common Ingredient Conversions:**
- 1 stick of butter = 1/2 cup = 113 grams
- 1 cup of flour = 120 grams
- 1 cup of sugar = 200 grams

6. **Oven Temperature Conversions:**
- Gas Mark 1 = 275°F = 140°C
- Gas Mark 2 = 300°F = 150°C
- Gas Mark 4 = 350°F = 180°C
- Gas Mark 6 = 400°F = 200°C
- Gas Mark 8 = 450°F = 230°C.

Made in the USA
Las Vegas, NV
15 November 2024

11870760R00066